Louise Erdrich

grew up in North Dakota and is of German-American and Chippewa descent. She is the author of a powerful quartet of novels, each self-contained: *Love Medicine*, *The Beet Queen*, *Tracks* and *The Bingo Palace* (all available in Flamingo paperback editions). She has published another volume of poetry, *Baptism of Desire*, a memoir of mothering, *The Blue Jay's Dance*, and is co-author with her husband, Michael Dorris, of the novel *The Crown of Columbus*. Her latest novel is *Tales of Burning Love* (1996).

ORIGINAL

LOUISE ERDRICH

Jacklight

Poems

Flamingo

An Imprint of HarperCollins*Publishers*

f l a m i n g o	The term 'Original' signifies publication direct into paperback with no preceding British hardback edition.
ORIGINAL	The Flamingo Original series publishes fine writing at an affordable price at the point of first publication.

Flamingo
an imprint of
HarperCollins*Publishers*
77–85 Fulham Palace Road,
Hammersmith, London W6 8JB

Published by Flamingo 1996
9 8 7 6 5 4 3 2 1

First published in the USA by
Henry Holt & Co. Inc. 1984

Copyright © Louise Erdrich 1984

Louise Erdrich asserts the moral right to
be identified as the author of this work

ISBN 0 00 654622 6

The author would like to thank The MacDowell Colony,
the Native American Studies Department at Dartmouth
College, and Yaddo Colony for the Arts for the time
and support to work on these poems.

Printed in Great Britain by
Caledonian International Book Manufacturing Ltd, Glasgow

All rights reserved. No part of this publication may be
reproduced, stored in a retrieval system, or transmitted,
in any form or by any means, electronic, mechanical,
photocopying, recording or otherwise, without the prior
permission of the publishers.

This book is sold subject to the condition that it shall not,
by way of trade or otherwise, be lent, re-sold, hired out or
otherwise circulated without the publisher's prior consent
in any form of binding or cover other than that in which it
is published and without a similar condition including this
condition being imposed on the subsequent purchaser.

For my parents

I would like to thank my teachers and friends,
Dick Corum, A. B. Paulson, Michael Martone, Joe Richardson,
Wendy Salinger, Mark Vinz, Judy Karasik, a fine
editor, and most of all, my husband Michael Dorris.

Contents

MYTHS

Jacklight

Jacklight

The same Chippewa word is used both for flirting and hunting game, while another Chippewa word connotes both using force in intercourse and also killing a bear with one's bare hands.

—R. W. Dunning
(1959) *Social and Economic Change Among the Northern Ojibwa*

We have come to the edge of the woods,
out of brown grass where we slept, unseen,
out of knotted twigs, out of leaves creaked shut,
out of hiding.

At first the light wavered, glancing over us.
Then it clenched to a fist of light that pointed,
searched out, divided us.
Each took the beams like direct blows the heart answers.
Each of us moved forward alone.

We have come to the edge of the woods,
drawn out of ourselves by this night sun,
this battery of polarized acids,
that outshines the moon.

We smell them behind it
but they are faceless, invisible.
We smell the raw steel of their gun barrels,
mink oil on leather, their tongues of sour barley.
We smell their mothers buried chin-deep in wet dirt.
We smell their fathers with scoured knuckles,
teeth cracked from hot marrow.
We smell their sisters of crushed dogwood, bruised apples,
of fractured cups and concussions of burnt hooks.

We smell their breath steaming lightly behind the jacklight.
We smell the itch underneath the caked guts on their clothes.
We smell their minds like silver hammers

cocked back, held in readiness
for the first of us to step into the open.

We have come to the edge of the woods,
out of brown grass where we slept, unseen,
out of leaves creaked shut, out of our hiding.
We have come here too long.

It is their turn now,
their turn to follow us. Listen,
they put down their equipment.
It is useless in the tall brush.
And now they take the first steps, not knowing
how deep the woods are and lightless.
How deep the woods are.

Runaways

A Love Medicine

For Lise

Still it is raining lightly
in Wahpeton. The pickup trucks
sizzle beneath the blue neon
bug traps of the dairy bar.

Theresa goes out in green halter and chains
that glitter at her throat.
This dragonfly, my sister,
she belongs more than I
to this night of rising water.

The Red River swells to take the bridge.
She laughs and leaves her man in his Dodge.
He shoves off to search her out.
He wears a long rut in the fog.

And later, at the crest of the flood,
when the pilings are jarred from their sockets
and pitch into the current,
she steps against the fistwork of a man.
She goes down in wet grass
and his boot plants its grin
among the arches of her face.

Now she feels her way home in the dark.
The white-violet bulbs of the streetlamps
are seething with insects,
and the trees lean down aching and empty.
The river slaps at the dike works, insistent.

I find her curled up in the roots of a cottonwood.
I find her stretched out in the park, where all night
the animals are turning in their cages.
I find her in a burnt-over ditch, in a field
that is gagging on rain,

sheets of rain sweep up down
to the river held tight against the bridge.

We see that now the moon is leavened and the water,
as deep as it will go,
stops rising. Where we wait for the night to take us
the rain ceases. *Sister, there is nothing
I would not do.*

Family Reunion

Ray's third new car in half as many years.
Full cooler in the trunk, Ray sogging the beer
as I solemnly chauffeur us through the bush
and up the backroads, hardly cowpaths and hub-deep in mud.
All day the sky lowers, clears, lowers again.
Somewhere in the bush near Saint John
there are uncles, a family, one mysterious brother
who stayed on the land when Ray left for the cities.
One week Ray is crocked. We've been through this before.
Even, as a little girl, hands in my dress,
Ah punka, you's my Debby, come and ki me.

Then the road ends in a yard full of dogs.
Them's Indian dogs, Ray says, lookit how they know me.
And they do seem to know him, like I do. His odor—
rank beef of fierce turtle pulled dripping from Metagoshe,
and the inflammable mansmell: hair tonic, ashes, alcohol.
Ray dances an old woman up in his arms.
Fiddles reel in the phonograph and I sink apart
in a corner, start knocking the Blue Ribbons down.
Four generations of people live here.
No one remembers Raymond Twobears.

So what. The walls shiver, the old house caulked with mud
sails back into the middle of Metagoshe.
A three-foot-long snapper is hooked on a troutline,
so mean that we do not dare wrestle him in
but tow him to shore, heavy as an old engine.
Then somehow Ray pries the beak open and shoves
down a cherry bomb. Lights the string tongue.

Headless and clenched in its armor, the snapper
is lugged home in the trunk for tomorrow's soup.
Ray rolls it beneath a bush in the backyard and goes in

to sleep his own head off. Tomorrow I find
that the animal has dragged itself someplace.
I follow torn tracks up a slight hill and over
into a small stream that deepens and widens into a marsh.

Ray finds his way back through the room into his arms.
When the phonograph stops, he slumps hard in his hands
and the boys and their old man fold him into the car
where he curls around his bad heart, hearing how it knocks
and rattles at the bars of his ribs to break out.

Somehow we find our way back. Uncle Ray
sings an old song to the body that pulls him
toward home. The gray fins that his hands have become
screw their bones in the dashboard. His face
has the odd, calm patience of a child who has always
let bad wounds alone, or a creature that has lived
for a long time underwater. And the angels come
lowering their slings and litters.

Indian Boarding School: The Runaways

Home's the place we head for in our sleep.
Boxcars stumbling north in dreams
don't wait for us. We catch them on the run.
The rails, old lacerations that we love,
shoot parallel across the face and break
just under Turtle Mountains. Riding scars
you can't get lost. Home is the place they cross.

The lame guard strikes a match and makes the dark
less tolerant. We watch through cracks in boards
as the land starts rolling, rolling till it hurts
to be here, cold in regulation clothes.
We know the sheriff's waiting at midrun
to take us back. His car is dumb and warm.
The highway doesn't rock, it only hums
like a wing of long insults. The worn-down welts
of ancient punishments lead back and forth.

All runaways wear dresses, long green ones,
the color you would think shame was. We scrub
the sidewalks down because it's shameful work.
Our brushes cut the stone in watered arcs
and in the soak frail outlines shiver clear
a moment, things us kids pressed on the dark
face before it hardened, pale, remembering
delicate old injuries, the spines of names and leaves.

Dear John Wayne

August and the drive-in picture is packed.
We lounge on the hood of the Pontiac
surrounded by the slow-burning spirals they sell
at the window, to vanquish the hordes of mosquitoes.
Nothing works. They break through the smoke screen for blood.

Always the lookout spots the Indians first,
spread north to south, barring progress.
The Sioux or some other Plains bunch
in spectacular columns, ICBM missiles,
feathers bristling in the meaningful sunset.

The drum breaks. There will be no parlance.
Only the arrows whining, a death-cloud of nerves
swarming down on the settlers
who die beautifully, tumbling like dust weeds
into the history that brought us all here
together: this wide screen beneath the sign of the bear.

The sky fills, acres of blue squint and eye
that the crowd cheers. His face moves over us,
a thick cloud of vengeance, pitted
like the land that was once flesh. Each rut,
each scar makes a promise: *It is*
not over, this fight, not as long as you resist.

Everything we see belongs to us.

A few laughing Indians fall over the hood
slipping in the hot spilled butter.
The eye sees a lot, John, but the heart is so blind.
Death makes us owners of nothing.
He smiles, a horizon of teeth
the credits reel over, and then the white fields

again blowing in the true-to-life dark.
The dark films over everything.
We get into the car
scratching our mosquito bites, speechless and small
as people are when the movie is done.
We are back in our skins.

How can we help but keep hearing his voice,
the flip side of the sound track, still playing:
Come on, boys, we got them
where we want them, drunk, running.
They'll give us what we want, what we need.
Even his disease was the idea of taking everything.
Those cells, burning, doubling, splitting out of their skins.

Rugaroo

For Heidi

He was the man who drank Vitalis
and sat up all night
with the mud puppies in the woodwork,
with the lights on in every room,
with the television, with the tap running,
with the fan blowing, with the icebox
sagged open, with the secondhand vacuum cleaner
sucking air.

He was the man who drank Sterno.
He was the man with the awful shakes.
He was the man with the bag of oranges
who took you home.

All night you could hear him in the woods coughing feathers.
Next morning he sat across from you pouring syrup
down his jacket.
His feet were the burnt stubs of brooms.

He was the man who cut rhubarb with a hatchet.
He wanted to keep you for good.
His arms cracked at the shoulders
and fell off like branches.
You threw them in a ditch.
You threw them behind the house.
They tangled around you and grew.

He was the man who couldn't sleep.
He went down into the cellar
and ate raw potatoes.
He blew up with gas.
And now he is the green light floating over the slough.
He is the one in the cattails at the edge of your dream.
He is the man who will not let you sleep.

Francine's Room

This is Tarsus, one place like anyplace else.
And this is my circuit, the rodeo, fair.
The farmboys blow through here in pickups, wild
as horses in their oat sacks.
The women wear spurs.
In the trailers the cattle are pounding for air.

My room is the same as last year. They always give me
end of the corridor, left, the top floor.
Privacy. Why not. I've been through here before.
I'm the town's best
customer. A minor attraction.
I buy from their stores. Remember this bureau—

battered wood, the fake drawer and split mirror?
And even the glass marks, ring within ring
of spilled drinks. When I sit here
the widest warped links have a center.
Strung out they're a year's worth of slack, a tether
that swings around the spine's dark pole

and swings back. Each time I return
something's different,
although there's a few I can always expect.
The cracks in the mirror: always more, never less.
The stains in the bedspread have spread.
And the rip in the window shade lets through more light,
strange light, since I come here to be in the dark.
Should be taped. A few things can be saved anyhow.
But I don't want to get into that.

I set up my pictures. Mother and Father,
stiffer, more blurred every year.
I turn them to the walls when there's customers, that

is the least I can do. What mending there is
occurs in small acts,
and after the fact of the damage,
when nothing is ever enough.
There is always the scar to remind me
that things were once perfect, at least

they were new. I first came here when I was a girl.
It surprised me, the things that two people could do
left alone in a room. Not long and I learned.
I learned what the selves are a man can disown
till he lets them to life in a room.

It's the region's hard winters, snowed in with the snow
half the year. I'd expect them to think up a few.
But nothing surprises me, not anymore.
The plumbing can only get worse with the cold.
It's true, even summers the water is foul
and flows slowly, a thin brown trickle by noon.

Heat pours in the west, freak waves of dry lightning
soak the whole town in a feverish light.
Beneath me, the tables of water have dropped
to unheard-of levels. It's been a long drought.
I bend my whole arm to the handle, the valve
yawns open but nothing comes out. What else should I
expect. Wrung cloth. The body washing in dust.

The Lady in the Pink Mustang

The sun goes down for hours, taking more of her along
than the night leaves her with.
A body moving in the dust
must shed its heavy parts in order to go on.

Perhaps you have heard of her, the Lady in the Pink Mustang,
whose bare lap is floodlit from under the dash,
who cruises beneath the high snouts of semis, reading
the blink of their lights. *Yes. Move Over. Now.*
or *How Much.* Her price shrinks into the dark.

She can't keep much trash in a Mustang,
and that's what she likes. Travel light. Don't keep
what does not have immediate uses. The road thinks ahead.
It thinks for her, a streamer from Bismarck to Fargo
bending through Minnesota to accommodate the land.

She won't carry things she can't use anymore.
Just a suit, sets of underwear, what you would expect
in a Pink Mustang. Things she could leave anywhere.

There is a point in the distance where the road meets itself,
where coming and going must kiss into one.
She is always at that place, seen from behind,
motionless, torn forward, living in a zone
all her own. It is like she has burned right through time,
the brand, the mark, owning the woman who bears it.

She owns them, not one will admit what they cannot
come close to must own them. She takes them along,
traveling light. It is what she must face every time
she is touched. The body disposable as cups.

To live, instead of turn, on a dime.
One light point that is so down in value.

Painting her nipples silver for a show, she is thinking
You out there. What do you know.

Come out of the dark where you're safe. Kissing these
bits of change, stamped out, ground to a luster,
is to kiss yourself away piece by piece
until we're even. Until the last
coin is rubbed for luck and spent.
I don't sell for nothing less.

Walking in the Breakdown Lane

Wind has stripped
the young plum trees
to a thin howl.
They are planted in squares
to keep the loose dirt from wandering.
Everything around me is crying to be gone.
The fields, the crops humming to be cut and done with.

Walking in the breakdown lane, margin of gravel,
between the cut swaths and the road to Fargo,
I want to stop, to lie down
in standing wheat or standing water.

Behind me thunder mounts as trucks of cattle
roar over, faces pressed to slats for air.
They go on, they go on without me.
They pound, pound and bawl,
until the road closes over them farther on.

Hunters

The Woods

At one time your touches were clothing enough.
Within these trees now I am different.
Now I wear the woods.

I lower a headdress of bent sticks and secure it.
I strap to myself a breastplate of clawed, roped bark.
I fit the broad leaves of sugar maples
to my hands, like mittens of blood.

Now when I say *come*,
and you enter the woods,
hunting some creature like the woman I was,
I surround you.

Light bleeds from the clearing. Roots rise.
Fluted molds burn blue in the falling light,
and you also know
the loneliness that you taught me with your body.

When you lay down in the grave of a slashed tree,
I cover you, as I always did;
this time you do not leave.

The Levelers

Again I see us walking toward the hen-fire, pale
ruff wavering among the trees,
a green fragile glow
that went dark when I touched it.
How could I have known.

Rocking you in sleep and you waking
to less of how we love
and the dream winding down,
I wanted to reverse that sure motion
that means to me *now we are going*.

Even stopping to let the world sway forward without us,
allowing the silence to clarify, loss
began to breathe a black soot in the glass. I knew then
an obscurity smokes
in the clearest of forms.

Caresses, the hand wearing the body, wearing down.
Already, in the palm, the first lines of erosion
are drinking. And the loving touch
seeks a still deeper source.
From the first, our own destruction was nursing at the heart.

Again I see us walking into the night trees.
Irreversible motion, but the branches are now lit within.
Husband, by the light of our bones we are going.
Beneath our own hands our bodies are leveling.

Train

Our bodies keep spilling their sweet, heavy freight
as the night goes.
The morning brings heavier snows
that settle around us, drifts in blind corners,
and a wind that recovers what falls.

Refusing to give up any part of my load,
I push it before me until the world fills
with voices. *Stop. Let it go. Now.*
I keep moving
although the weight makes me slow.

Tunnels that the body strikes open in air.
Bridges that shiver across
every water I come to.
And always the light
I was born with, driving everything before it.

Here is the charge I carried, the ballast
I chose to go down with,
the ponderous soul.
Here is the light I was born with, love.
Here is the bleak radiance that levels the world.

Captivity

He (my captor) gave me a bisquit, which I put in my pocket, and not daring to eat it,
buried it under a log, fearing he had put something in it to make me love him.
   —from the narrative of the captivity of Mrs. Mary
     Rowlandson, who was taken prisoner by the Wampanoag
     when Lancaster, Massachusetts, was destroyed, in the year 1676

The stream was swift, and so cold
I thought I would be sliced in two.
But he dragged me from the flood
by the ends of my hair.
I had grown to recognize his face.
I could distinguish it from the others.
There were times I feared I understood
his language, which was not human,
and I knelt to pray for strength.

We were pursued! By God's agents
or pitch devils I did not know.
Only that we must march.
Their guns were loaded with swan shot.
I could not suckle and my child's wail
put them in danger.
He had a woman
with teeth black and glittering.
She fed the child milk of acorns.
The forest closed, the light deepened.

I told myself that I would starve
before I took food from his hands
but I did not starve.
One night
he killed a deer with a young one in her
and gave me to eat of the fawn.
It was so tender,
the bones like the stems of flowers,

that I followed where he took me.
The night was thick. He cut the cord
that bound me to the tree.

After that the birds mocked.
Shadows gaped and roared
and the trees flung down
their sharpened lashes.
He did not notice God's wrath.
God blasted fire from half-buried stumps.
I hid my face in my dress, fearing He would burn us all
but this, too, passed.

Rescued, I see no truth in things.
My husband drives a thick wedge
through the earth, still it shuts
to him year after year.
My child is fed of the first wheat.
I lay myself to sleep
on a Holland-laced pillowbeer.
I lay to sleep.
And in the dark I see myself
as I was outside their circle.

They knelt on deerskins, some with sticks,
and he led his company in the noise
until I could no longer bear
the thought of how I was.
I stripped a branch
and struck the earth,
in time, begging it to open
to admit me
as he was
and feed me honey from the rock.

Chahinkapa Zoo

It is spring. Even here
the bears emerge from poured caverns.
Already their cubs have been devoured
by the feather-footed lynx caged next door.
The mad eagle in its gazebo of chicken wire
croaks at fish. The bull elk lowers
its lashes like a virgin
to take the bread.

Geese hurtle from the sky
black and garrulous.
It is time for the snappers
to drag over tarred roads to their nesting ground.
They roll against the new fence like tanks.
They founder but will not turn. They die,
chain link knotted in their beaks,
heavy with the ancient life.

Each noon the town siren blows wild
and the yellow-eyed wolf answers
Run with me.

The King of Owls

*It is said that playing cards were invented in 1392 to cure the French king,
Charles VI, of madness. The suits in some of the first card packs consisted of
Doves, Peacocks, Ravens, and Owls.*

They say I am excitable! How could
I not scream? The Swiss monk's tonsure
spun till it blurred yet his eyes were still.
I snapped my gaiter, hard, to stuff back

my mirth. Lords, he then began to speak.
Indus catarum, he said, *presenting the game of cards
in which the state of the world is excellent described
and figured.* He decked his mouth

as they do, a solemn stitch, and left cards
in my hands. I cast them down.
What need have I for amusement?
My brain's a park. Yet your company

plucked them from the ground and began to play.
Lords, I wither. The monk spoke right,
the mealy wretch. The sorry patterns show
the deceiving constructions of your minds.

I have made the Deuce of Ravens my sword
falling through your pillows and rising,
the wing blades still running
with the jugular blood. Your bodies lurch

through the steps of an unpleasant dance.
No lutes play. I have silenced the lutes!
I keep watch in the clipped, convulsed garden.
I must have silence, to hear the messenger's footfall

in my brain. For I am the King of Owls.
Where I float no shadow falls.
I have hungers, such terrible hungers, you cannot know.
Lords, I sharpen my talons on your bones.

Painting of a White Gate and Sky

For Betsy

There is no one in the picture
so you must enter it.
Your dress held together with bent pins.
You must enter
with your heart of gray snow.

There is no one in the blank left corner
so you must stand there.
You with your wrists chained,
with your stomach locked up.
You with emptiness tapping
sorrow's code
in its cage of bone.

The steps are grown over with sharp blades.
No one has been there.
You are the first one.
Desperate, proper,
your heels leave deep punctures.

You with breath failing.
You with your mother's ring.
With your belt undone.
You with your mind of twisted ferns.

There is no one at the gate
so you must stand there.
You with your picked-over heart.
You with shoulders of cracked glass.
With hands falling open.
You with nobody.

It is a gate no one ever pushed open,
a gate that stands alone,

swung shut before the stars
were strung up in the black net.

There is no one beyond the gate.
There is no one to watch you.
There is no one to see grief unloading like train cars.

Go there you chained one
You heels that leave wounds
You sister
You heart of gray snow.

Night Sky

Lunar eclipse, for Michael

I

Arcturus, the bear driver,
shines on the leash of hunting dogs.
Do you remember how the woman becomes a bear
because her husband has run in sadness
to the forest of stars?

She soaks the bear hide
until it softens to fit her body.
She ties the skinning boards over her heart.
She goes out, digs stumps,
smashes trees to test her power,
then breaks into a dead run
and hits the sky like a truck.

We are watching the moon
when this bear woman pulls herself
arm over arm into the tree of heaven.
We see her shadow clasp the one rusted fruit.
Her thick paw swings. The world dims.
We are alone here on earth
with the ragged breath of our children
coming and going in the old wool blankets.

II

Does she ever find him?
The sky is full of pits and snagged deadfalls.
She sleeps in shelters he's made of jackpine,
eats the little black bones
of birds he's roasted in cookfires.
She even sees him once
bending to drink from his own lips
in the river of starlight.

The truth is she cannot approach him
in the torn face and fur
stinking of shit and leather.
She is a real bear now,
licking bees from her paws, plunging
her snout in anthills,
rolling mad in the sour valleys
of skunk cabbage!

III

He knows she is there,
eyeing him steadily from the hornbeam
as she used to across the table.
He asks for strength
to leave his body at the river,
to leave it cradled in its sad arms
while he wanders in oiled muscles,
bear heft, shag, and acorn fat.
He goes to her, heading
for the open,
the breaking moon.

IV

Simple
to tear free
stripped and shining
to ride through crossed firs

The Butcher's Wife

FOR MARY KORLL

The Butcher's Wife

1

Once, my braids swung heavy as ropes.
Men feared them like the gallows.
Night fell
When I combed them out.
No one could see me in the dark.

Then I stood still
Too long and the braids took root.
I wept, so helpless.
The braids tapped deep and flourished.

A man came by with an ox on his shoulders.
He yoked it to my apron
And pulled me from the ground.
From that time on I wound the braids around my head
So that my arms would be free to tend him.

2

He could lift a grown man by the belt with his teeth.
In a contest, he'd press a whole hog, a side of beef.
He loved his highballs, his herring, and the attentions of women.
He died pounding his chest with no last word for anyone.

The gin vessels in his face broke and darkened. I traced them
Far from that room into Bremen on the Sea.
The narrow streets twisted down to the piers.
And far off, in the black, rocking water, the lights of trawlers
Beckoned, like the heart's uncertain signals,
Faint, and final.

3

Of course I planted a great, full bush of roses on his grave.
Who else would give the butcher roses but his wife?
Each summer, I am reminded of the heart surging from his vest,
Mocking all the high stern angels
By pounding for their spread skirts.

The flowers unfurl, offering themselves,
And I hear his heart pound on the earth like a great fist,
Demanding another round of the best wine in the house.
Another round, he cries, and another round all summer long,
Until the whole damn world reels toward winter drunk.

That Pull from the Left

Butch once remarked to me how sinister it was
alone, after hours, in the dark of the shop
to find me there hunched over two weeks' accounts
probably smoked like a bacon from all those Pall-Malls.

Odd comfort when the light goes, the case lights left on
and the rings of baloney, the herring, the parsley,
arranged in the strict, familiar ways.

Whatever intactness holds animals up
has been carefully taken, what's left are the parts.
Just look in the cases, all counted and stacked.

Step-and-a-Half Waleski used to come to the shop
and ask for the cheap cut, she would thump, sniff, and finger.
This one too old. This one here for my supper.
Two days and you do notice change in the texture.

I have seen them the day before slaughter.
Knowing of the outcome from the moment they enter
the chute, the eye rolls, blood is smeared on the lintel.
Mallet or bullet they lunge toward their darkness.

But something queer happens when the heart is delivered.
When a child is born, sometimes the left hand is stronger.
You can train it to fail, still the knowledge is there.
That is the knowledge in the hand of a butcher

that adds to its weight. Otto Kröger could fell
a dray horse with one well-placed punch to the jaw,
and yet it is well known how thorough he was.

He never sat down without washing his hands,
and he was a maker, his sausage was *echt*

so that even Waleski had little complaint.
Butch once remarked there was no one so deft
as my Otto. So true, there is great tact involved
in parting the flesh from the bones.

How we cling to the bones. Each joint is a web
of small tendons and fibers. He knew what I meant
when I told him I felt something pull from the left,
and how often it clouded the day before slaughter.

Something queer happens when the heart is delivered.

Clouds

The furnace is stoked. I'm loaded
on gin. One bottle in the clinkers
hidden since spring
when Otto took the vow
and ceremoniously poured
the rotgut, the red-eye, the bootlegger's brew
down the scoured steel sink,
overcoming the reek
of oxblood.
That was one promise he kept.
He died two weeks after, not a drop crossed his lips
in the meantime. I know
now he kept some insurance,
one bottle at least
against his own darkness.
I'm here, anyway, to give it some use.

From the doorway the clouds pass me through.
The town stretches to fields. The six avenues
crossed by seventeen streets,
the tick, tack, and toe
of boxes and yards
settle into the dark.
Dogs worry their chains.
Men call to their mothers
and finish. The women sag into the springs.
What kind of thoughts, Mary Kröger, are these?
With a headful of spirits,
how else can I think?
Under so many clouds,
such hooded and broken
old things. They go on

simply folding, unfolding, like sheets
hung to dry and forgotten.

And no matter how careful I watch them,
they take a new shape,
escaping my concentrations,
they slip and disperse
and extinguish themselves.
They melt before I half unfathom their forms.
Just as fast, a few bones
disconnecting beneath us.
It is too late, I fear, to call these things back.
Not in this language.
Not in this life.

I know it. The tongue is unhinged by the sauce.
But these clouds, creeping toward us
each night while the milk
gets scorched in the pan,
great soaked loaves of bread
are squandering themselves in the west.

Look at them: Proud, unpausing.
Open and growing, we cannot destroy them
or stop them from moving
down each avenue,
the dogs turn on their chains,
children feel through the windows.
What else should we feel our way through—

We lay our streets over
the deepest cries of the earth
and wonder why everything comes down to this:

The days pile and pile.
The bones are too few
and too foreign to know.
Mary, you do not belong here at all.

Sometimes I take back in tears this whole town.
Let everything be how it could have been, once:
a land that was empty and perfect as clouds.
But this is the way people are.
All that appears to us empty,
We fill.
What is endless and simple,
We carve, and initial,
and narrow
roads plow through the last of the hills
where our gravestones rear small
black vigilant domes.
Our friends, our family, the dead of our wars,
deep in this strange earth
we want to call ours.

Shelter

My four adopted sons in photographs
wear solemn black. Their faces comprehend
their mother's death, an absence in a well
of empty noise, and Otto strange and lost.
Her name was Mary also, Mary Kröger.
Two of us have lived and one is gone.
Her hair was blond; it floated back in wings,
and still you see her traces in the boys:
bright hair and long, thin, knotted woman's hands.
I knew her, Mary Kröger, and we were bosom friends.
All graves are shelters for our mislaid twins.

Otto was for many years her husband,
and that's the way I always thought of him.
I nursed her when she sickened and the cure
fell through at Rochester. The healing bath
that dropped her temperature, I think, too fast.
I was in attendance at her death:
She sent the others out. She rose and gripped my arm
and tried to make me promise that I'd care
for Otto and the boys. I had to turn away
as my own mother had when her time came.
How few do not return in memory
and make us act in ways we can't explain.
I could not lie to ease her, living, dying.
All graves are full of such accumulation.
And yet, the boys were waiting in New York
to take the first boat back to Otto's folks
in Germany, prewar, dark powers were at work,
and Otto asked me on the westbound bus
to marry him. I could not tell him no—
We help our neighbors out. I loved him though

It took me several years to know I did
from that first time he walked in to deliver
winter food. Through Father Adler's kitchen,
he shouldered half an ox like it was bread
and looked at me too long for simple greeting.
This is how our lives complete themselves,
as effortless as weather, circles blaze
in ordinary days, and through our waking selves
they reach, to touch our true and sleeping speech.

So I took up with Otto, took the boys
and watched for them, and made their daily bread
from what the grocer gave them in exchange
for helping him. It's hard to tell you how
they soon became so precious I got sick
from worry, and woke up for two months straight
and had to check them, sleeping, in their beds,
and had to watch and see each breathe or move
before I could regain my sleep again.
All graves are pregnant with our nearest kin.

The Slow Sting of Her Company

Otto brought one sister from that town
they never talk about. His father shook
one great red fist, a bludgeon, in the air
behind them as dry sparks released the wheels.
I pictured him, still standing there, now shrunk—
a carved root pickling in its own strong juice.
They speak his name and wipe it from their lips.
                    Proud Hilda hides his picture
                    in a drawer with underskirts.

Tall Hilda sniffed and twisted that gold chain
my Otto gave her. Other, lesser men
have gifted her with more impressive things.
She keeps them in a drawer with towels and sheets.
I came upon a sentimental locket,
embossed with words, initials interfixed
within the breasts of dour, molting swans.
                    Proud Hilda cracked it open,
                    smiled, and clicked it shut.

How many men had begged her heavy hand
I do not know. I think I loved her too
in ways that I am not sure how to tell—
I reached one day to gather back her hair:
wild marigold. I touched one hidden ear
and drew my fingers, burning, from the stone
that swung a cold light from the polished lobe.
                    Tall Hilda took my hand in hers and kissed
                    the palm, and closed that mark inside my fist.

She lived alone and thickened in that town,
refusing company for weeks on end.
We left food at her door; she took it in;
her dull lamp deepened as the night wore on.

I went to her when everything was wrong.
We sat all evening talking children, men.
She laughed at me, and said it was my ruin:
        My giving till I dropped.
        Live blood let down the drain.

I never let her know how those words cut
me serious—her questioning my life. One night
a slow thing came, provoked by weariness,
to cram itself up every slackened nerve;
as if my body were a whining hive
and each cell groaning with a sweet thick lead—
I turned and struck at Otto in our bed;
all night, all night the poison, till I swarmed
        back empty to his cold
        and dreaming arms.

Here Is a Good Word for Step-and-a-Half Waleski

At first we all wondered what county or town
she had come from. Quite soon it was clear to us all
that was better unquestioned, and better unknown.
Who wanted to hear what had happened or failed
to occur. Why the dry wood had not taken fire.
Much less, why the dogs were unspeakably disturbed

when she ground the cold cinders that littered our walk
with her run-to-ground heels. That Waleski approached
with a swiftness uncommon for one of her age.
Even spiders spun clear of her lengthening shadow.
Her headlong occurrence unnerved even Otto
who wrapped up the pork rinds like they were glass trinkets
and saluted her passage with a good stiff drink.

But mine is a good word for Step-and-a-Half Waleski.
Scavenger, bone picker, lived off our alleys
when all we threw out were the deadliest scrapings
from licked-over pots. And even that hurt.
And for whatever one of us laughed in her face,
at least two prayed in secret, went home half afraid
of the mirror, what possible leavings they'd find there.

But mine is a good word, and even that hurts.
A rhyme-and-a-half for a woman of parts,
because someone must pare the fruit soft to the core
into slivers, must wrap the dead bones in her skirts
and lay these things out on her table, and fit
each oddment to each to resemble a life.

Portrait of the Town Leonard

I thought I saw him look my way and crossed
my breast before I could contain myself.
Beneath those glasses, thick as lead-barred windows,
his eyes ran through his head, the double barrels
of an old gun, sick on its load, the trigger held
in place by one thin metal bow.

Going toward the Catholic church, whose twin
white dunce caps speared the clouds for offering,
we had to pass him on the poured stone bridge.
For nickels we could act as though we'd not
been offered stories. How these all turned out
we knew, each one, just how the river eats
within its course the line of reasoning.

He went, each morning, to the first confession.
The sulking curtains bit their lips behind him.
Still those in closer pews could hear the sweet
and limber sins he'd made up on the spot.
I saw a few consider, and take note—
procedural. They'd try them out at home.

And once, a windless August, when the sun
released its weight and all the crops were burned,
he kept watch as the river thickened. Land
grew visibly and reeked to either side,
till windowed hulks, forgotten death cars reared
where dark fish leapt, and gaped, and snatched the air.

Leonard Commits Redeeming Adulteries
with All the Women in Town

When I take off my glasses, these eyes are dark magnets
that draw the world into my reach.
First the needles, as I walk the quiet streets,
work their way from their cushions of dust.
The nails in the rafters twist laboriously out
and the oven doors drop
an inch open.
The sleep-smell of yesterday's baking
rises in the mouth.
A good thing.

The streetlamps wink off just at dawn,
still they bend their stiff necks like geese drinking.
My vision is drinking in the star-littered lawn.
When the porch ivy weaves to me—
Now is the time.
Women put down their coffee cups, all over town.
Men drift down the sidewalks, thinking,
What did she want?
But it is too late for husbands.
Their wives do not question
what it is that dissolves
all reserve. Why they suddenly think of cracked Leonard.

They uncross themselves, forsaking
all protection. They long to be opened and known
because the secret is perishable, kept, and desire
in love with its private ruin.
I open my hands and they come to me, now.
In our palms dark instructions that cannot be erased,
only followed, only known along the way.

And it is right, oh women of the town, it is *right*.
Your mouths, like the seals of important documents
break for me, destroying the ring's raised signature,
the cracked edges melting to mine.

Leonard Refuses to Atone

The moon comes up, a white cow
grazing on limbo.
Today in the confessional I yelled,
Father, I am the deaf one, absolve me
in a voice I can hear.
But as usual, he mumbled in the curtain
and the saints cast their eyes
past me, into the cold space of the loft
when I knelt at their feet.

What sins have I done
that you should forsake me?
Again, I asked loudly.
The saints are far deafer than I.
Their ears, curls of plaster,
have grown closed from listening
to the organ's unceasing low sobs.

I sit where the moon rides up,
swollen and tender,
the beast of my burdens. Her back is broad
enough to carry my penance and yours.
When she moans, the whole sky
falls open.
My weight has done this.
My life an act of contrition
for the sins of a whole town.

But now, when I let the weight fall,
she arches, a slender thing
shot from a quiver.
Oh white deer hunted into a cloud,
I was your child, now I leap down,

relaxed into purpose,
my body cleaves through the air like a star.

Make your wishes, small children.
You others, make vows,
quickly, before I snuff myself out
and become the dark thing
that walks among you,
pure, deaf, and full
of my own ingenious sins.

Unexpected Dangers

I'm much the worse for wear, it's double true.
Too many incidents
a man might misconstrue—
my conduct, for a lack of innocence.

I seem to get them crazed or lacking sense
in the first place.
Ancient, solid gents
I sit by on the bus because they're safe,

get me going, coming, with their canes,
or what is worse,
the spreading stains
across the seat. I recognize at once

just what they're up to, rustling in their coats.
There was a priest,
the calmer sort,
his cassock flowing down from neck to feet.

We got to talking and I brushed his knee
by accident,
and dutifully,
he took my hand and put it back

not quite where it belonged; his judgment
was not that exact.
I underwent
a kind of odd conversion from his act.

They do call minds like mine one-track.
One track is all you need
to understand
their loneliness, then bite the hand that feeds

upon you, in a terrible blind grief.

My Name Repeated on the Lips of the Dead

Last night, my dreams were full of Otto's best friends.
I sat in the kitchen, wiping the heavy silver,
and listened to the losses, tough custom, and fouled accounts
of the family bootlegger, county sheriff:
Rudy J. V. Jacklitch, who sat just beside me,
wiping his wind-cracked hands
with lard smeared on a handkerchief.

Our pekinese-poodle went and darkened his best wool trousers,
and he leapt up, yelling for a knife!

These are the kinds of friends
I had to tend in those days:
great, thick men, devouring
Fleisch, Spaetzle, the very special
potato salad for which I dice
onions so fine they are invisible.

Rudy J. V. Jacklitch was a bachelor, but he cared
for his mother, a small spider of a woman—all fingers.
She covered everything, from the kettle to the radio,
with a doily. The whole house
dripped with lace, frosting fell
from each surface in fantastic shapes.
When Otto died, old Rudy came by
with a couple jugs for the mourners' supper.
He stayed on past midnight, every night the month after
he would bring me a little something
to put the night away.

After a short while I knew his purpose.
His glance slipped as the evening
and the strong drink wore on.
Playing cribbage I always won,
a sure sign he was distracted.

I babbled like a talking bird,
never let him say the words
I knew were in him.

Then one night he came by,
already loaded to the gills,
rifle slung in the back window
of his truck: *Going out
to shoot toads*. He was peeved
with me. I'd played him all wrong.
He said his mother *knew just what I was*.

The next thing I heard that blurred night
was that Rudy drove his light truck
through the side of a barn,
and that among the living
he stayed long enough
to pronounce my name, like a curse
through the rage and foam of his freed blood.

So I was sure, for a time and a time after,
that Rudy carried
my name down to hell on his tongue
like a black coin.

I would wake, in the deepest of places,
and hear my name called.
My name like a strange new currency they read:
Mary Kröger
with its ring of the authentic
when dropped
or struck between their fingers.

How I feared to have it whispered in their mouths!

Mary Kröger
growing softer and thinner
till it dissolved
like a wafer under all that polishing.

A Mother's Hell

The Widow Jacklitch

All night, all night, the cat wants out again.
I've locked her in the kitchen where she tears
From wall to wall. Her bullet head leaves marks;
She swings from tablecloths, dislodges pots.
When Rudy was alive the cat was all
You ever could have wanted in a child, it sat so still
And diligently sucked its whiskers clean. I cram
A doily in my mouth to still the scream.

All night the sweethearts dandle in the weeds.
It's terrible, the little bleats they make
Outside my window. Girls not out of braids
Walk by. I see their fingers hike their skirts
Way up their legs. I say it's dirt.
The cat's got rubbage on her brain
As well. She backs on anything that's stiff.
I try to keep the pencils out of reach.

That Kröger widow practiced what she'd preach
A mile a minute. If she was a cat
I'd drown her in a tub of boiling fat
And nail her up like suet, out in back
Where birds fly down to take their chance.
I don't like things with beaks. I don't
Like anything that makes a beating sound.

Beat, beat, all night they hammered at the truck
With bats. But he had locked himself
In stubbornly as when a boy. I'd knock
Until my knuckles scabbed and bled
And blue paint scraped into the wounds. He'd laugh
Behind his door. I'd hear him pant and thrill.
A mother's hell. But I'd feel the good blindness stalk
Us together. Son and mother world without end forever.

The Book of Water

After we were done with the wreaths, the dirt and stone,
the neighbors came, took the boys, and left the heavy loaves
I wrapped and stored. The kitchen clock
traveled forward on its hidden wheels.
I went through the rooms and turned the shadows to the walls.

Then by the light of whiskey, I combed my braids down,
and entered the gray waves of a lake threatened by storm.
Long bitterns and herons rose crying from the surface
that never changed, reflecting a sky cast of a single piece.

And then the long birds walked up on the shore, and I saw
the water was a great book that opened and turned forward,
erasing the herons' tracks before I read and understood.

It was a whirl of rain and pages, a terrible amount of words.
There was a meaning not even Otto could have lifted in his arms.
But that night I was relentless as the waves, and I went down.
My arms pulling water were written over with scars.

At the bottom, I would learn to read the writing in that book.
And if my page was worn and creased, I would tear it out myself.

To Otto, in Forgetfulness

First I forget
your voice in my hair, arms
thick as stovepipes, the bad weather
of our wedding day.

Your voice
thick blood pudding all night,
the dogs bawled in the yard,
the heat lightning.

Then I forget where I have hidden your hands,
rolled up in my apron or baked in black loaves.
I forget the old stories
they told me.

The words fell together one night,
and each night the dark story
of the body, we told
another way. Turn away

from me. Otto
F. Kröger. I do not
remember your voice in my hair.
Mary willst du, meine Kleine, noch wieder.

My little bitch,
black Dorra, I forget
how she followed, giving litter
after litter to the well.
Dogs live well

in the house
of a butcher and we loved them.
All evening Dorra slept in your lap
and even after the funeral

she refused the lean scrap I did feed her.
They say a dog pines for its master.
I forget just what
happened

small shadow
of your passing.
I forget.

New Vows

The night was clean as the bone of a rabbit blown hollow.
I cast my hood of dogskin
away, and my shirt of nettles.
Three years had been enough. I left my darkened house.

The trick was in living that death to its source.
When it happened, I wandered toward more than I was.

Widowed by men, I married the dark firs,
as if I were walking in sleep toward their arms,
I drank, without fear or desire,
this odd fire.

Now shadows move freely within me as words.
These are eternal: these stunned, loosened verbs.
And I can't tell you yet
how truly I belong

to the hiss and shift of wind,
these slow, variable mouths
through which, at certain times, I speak in tongues.

Myths

I Was Sleeping Where the Black Oaks Move

We watched from the house
as the river grew, helpless
and terrible in its unfamiliar body.
Wrestling everything into it,
the water wrapped around trees
until their life-hold was broken.
They went down, one by one,
and the river dragged off their covering.

Nests of the herons, roots washed to bones,
snags of soaked bark on the shoreline:
a whole forest pulled through the teeth
of the spillway. Trees surfacing
singly, where the river poured off
into arteries for fields below the reservation.

When at last it was over, the long removal,
they had all become the same dry wood.
We walked among them, the branches
whitening in the raw sun.
Above us drifted herons,
alone, hoarse-voiced, broken,
settling their beaks among the hollows.

Grandpa said, *These are the ghosts of the tree people,*
moving above us, unable to take their rest.

Sometimes now, we dream our way back to the heron dance.
Their long wings are bending the air
into circles through which they fall.
They rise again in shifting wheels.
How long must we live in the broken figures
their necks make, narrowing the sky.

The Strange People

*The antelope are strange people . . . they are beautiful to look at, and
yet they are tricky. We do not trust them. They appear and disappear;
they are like shadows on the plains. Because of their great beauty, young
men sometimes follow the antelope and are lost forever. Even if those
foolish ones find themselves and return, they are never again right in their
heads.*
> —Pretty Shield, Medicine Woman of the Crows,
> transcribed and edited by Frank Linderman (1932)

All night I am the doe, breathing
his name in a frozen field,
the small mist of the word
drifting always before me.

And again he has heard it
and I have gone burning
to meet him, the jacklight
fills my eyes with blue fire;
the heart in my chest
explodes like a hot stone.

Then slung like a sack
in the back of his pickup,
I wipe the death scum
from my mouth, sit up laughing,
and shriek in my speeding grave.

Safely shut in the garage,
when he sharpens his knife
and thinks to have me, like that,
I come toward him,
a lean gray witch,
through the bullets that enter and dissolve.

I sit in his house
drinking coffee till dawn,
and leave as frost reddens on hubcaps,
crawling back into my shadowy body.
All day, asleep in clean grasses,
I dream of the one who could really wound me.

The Lefavor Girls

All autumn, black plums
split and dropped from the boughs.
We gathered the sweetness
and sealed it in jars,
loading the cupboards and cellar.

At night we went under the bedclothes, laden
beyond what the arms were meant to carry alone,
and we dreamed that with our shirts off
in the quarry, the cool water
came under to bear us away.

That season our sleep grew around us
as if from the walls
a dense snow fell and formed
other bodies, and the voices
of men who melted into us,
and children who drifted, lost, looking for home.

After the long rains, the land gone bare,
we walked out again to the windbreaks.
White crowns of the plum trees
were filling the purple throats of the iris.

We lay in the grass,
the bees drinking in tongues,
and already the brittle hum of the locust
in the red wheat, growing.

Again, the year come full circle, the men
came knocking in the fields,
headfuls of blackened seeds,
and the husking, scorched mountains of sunflowers.

We went closed, still golden, among the harvesters.
Shifting the load from arm to arm,
they drove us into town.
We shook out our dresses and hair, oh then

There was abundance come down
in the face of the coming year.
We held ourselves into
the wind, our bodies
broke open, and the snow began falling.

It fell until the world was filled up, and filled again,
until it rose past all the limits we could have known.

Three Sisters

Arlene wore the eyes of an old man around her neck.
Scratched porcelain, washed down
with the hot lye of his breath.

Dalona rode love like a ship in light wind.
The sails of her body unfurled at a touch.
No one could deny her safe passage, safe harbor.

Thedda, the youngest, was shut like a bell.
The white thorns of silence prickled in each bush
where she walked, and the grass stopped growing where she stood.

One year the three sisters came out of their rooms,
swaying like the roses that papered their walls.
They walked, full grown, into the heart of the town.

Young men broke their eyes against their eyes of stone,
and singed their long tongues
on the stunned flames of their mouths.

It was in late August, in the long year of drought.
The pool halls were winnowed and three men drew lots
to marry the sisters, all six in a great house.

On the night of the wedding the wind rose on a glass stem.
The clouds lowered in live heat.
We tethered our dogs.

Some swore they saw a hoop of lightning dance down in their yard.
Toward dawn, we felt the weight of lead sinkers in our bones,
walked out, and caught the first, fast drops on our tongues.

Whooping Cranes

For Mary Gourneau

Our souls must be small as mice
to fit through the hole of heaven.
All the time it is shrinking
over Pembina.

The newborn cried across the road
night and day until they buried
its mother at the Mission.
You found it in a ditch
sucking tea from a bottle   ·
and took him home. This boy grew
strange and secret among the others,
killing crows with his bare hands
and kissing his own face in the mirror.

One year everything dried up.
You held the boy toward heaven
so that his mother could see
you had managed to keep him fat.
Bands of hot dust were lifting.
Seed wings burnt
off the boxelders.
When the white cranes sailed over
trumpeting the boy's name
you let go
and he flew into their formation.

They were the last flight.
Their wings scraped the clouds dead white.
Their breasts were arks.
Their beaks were swords that barred the gate.
And the sky closed after them.

Old Man Potchikoo

The Birth of Potchikoo

You don't have to believe this, I'm not asking you to.

But Potchikoo claims that his father is the sun in heaven that shines down on us all.

There was a very pretty Chippewa girl working in a field once. She was digging potatoes for a farmer someplace around Pembina when suddenly the wind blew her dress up around her face and wrapped her apron so tightly around her arms that she couldn't move. She lay helplessly in the dust with her potato sack, this poor girl, and as she lay there she felt the sun shining down very steadily upon her.

Then she felt something else. You know what. I don't have to say it. She cried out for her mother.

This girl's mother came running and untangled her daughter's clothes. When she freed the girl, she saw that there were tears in her daughter's eyes. Bit by bit, the mother coaxed out the story. After the girl told what had happened to her, the mother just shook her head sadly.

"I don't know what we can expect now," she said.

Well nine months passed and he was born looking just like a potato with tough warty skin and a puckered round shape. All the ladies came to visit the girl and left saying things behind their hands.

"That's what she gets for playing loose in the potato fields," they said.

But the girl didn't care what they said after a while because she used to go and stand alone in a secret clearing in the woods and let the sun shine steadily upon her. Sometimes she took her little potato boy. She noticed when the sun shone on him he grew and became a little more human-looking.

One day the girl fell asleep in the sun with her potato boy next to her. The sun beat down so hard on him that he had an enormous spurt of growth. When the girl woke up, her son was fully grown. He said goodbye to his mother then, and went out to see what was going on in the world.

Potchikoo Marries

After he had several adventures, the potato boy took the name Potchikoo and decided to try married life.

I'll just see what it's like for a while, he thought, and then I'll start wandering again.

How very inexperienced he was!

He took the train to Minneapolis to find a wife and as soon as he got off he saw her. She was a beautiful Indian girl standing at the door to a little shop where they sold cigarettes and pipe tobacco. How proud she looked! How peaceful. She was so lovely that she made Potchikoo shy. He could hardly look at her.

Potchikoo walked into the store and bought some cigarettes. He lit one up and stuck it between the beautiful woman's lips. Then he stood next to her, still too shy to look at her, until he smelled smoke. He saw that she had somehow caught fire.

"Oh I'll save you!" cried Potchikoo.

He grabbed his lady love and ran with her to the lake, which was, handily, across the street. He threw her in. At first he was afraid she would drown but soon she floated to the surface and kept floating away from Potchikoo. This made him angry.

"Trying to run away already!" he shouted.

He leaped in to catch her. But he had forgotten that he couldn't swim. So Potchikoo had to hang on to his wooden sweetheart while she drifted slowly all the way across the lake. When they got to the other side of the lake, across from Minneapolis, they were in wilderness. As soon as the wooden girl touched the shore she became alive and jumped up and dragged Potchikoo out of the water.

"I'll teach you to shove a cigarette between my lips like that," she said, beating him with her fists, which were still hard as wood. "Now that you're my husband you'll do things my way!"

That was how Potchikoo met and married Josette. He was married to her all his life. After she had made it clear what she expected of her husband, Josette made a little toboggan of cut saplings and tied him upon it. Then she decided she never wanted to see Minneapolis again. She wanted to live in the hills. That is why she dragged Potchikoo all the way back across Minnesota to the Turtle Mountains, where they spent all the years of their wedded bliss.

How Potchikoo Got Old

As a young man, Potchikoo sometimes embarrassed his wife by breaking wind during Holy Mass. It was for this reason that Josette whittled him a little plug out of ash wood and told him to put it in that place before he entered Saint Ann's church.

Potchikoo did as she asked, and even said a certain charm over the plug so that it would not be forced out, no matter what. Then the two of them entered the church to say their prayers.

That Sunday, Father Belcourt was giving a special sermon on the ascension of the Lord Christ to heaven. It happened in the twinkling of an eye, he said, with no warning, because Christ was more pure than air. How surprised everyone was to see, as Father Belcourt said this, the evil scoundrel Potchikoo rising from his pew!

His hands were folded, and his closed eyes and meek face wore a look of utter piety. He didn't even seem to realize he was rising, he prayed so hard.

Up and up he floated, still in the kneeling position, until he reached the dark blue vault of the church. He seemed to inflate, too, until he looked larger than life to the people. They were on the verge of believing it a miracle when all of a sudden it happened. Bang! Even with the charm the little ash-wood plug could not contain the wind of Potchikoo. Out it popped, and Potchikoo went buzzing and sputtering around the church the way balloons do when children let go of the ends.

Holy Mass was canceled for a week so the church could be aired out, but to this day a faint scent still lingers and Potchikoo, sadly enough, was shriveled by his sudden collapse and flight through the air. For when Josette picked him up to bring home, she found that he was now wrinkled and dry like an old man.

The Death of Potchikoo

Once there were three stones sitting in a patch of soft slough mud. Each of these stones had the smooth round shape of a woman's breast, but no one had ever noticed this—that is, not until Old Man Potchikoo walked through the woods. He was the type who always noticed this kind of thing. As soon as he saw the three stones, Potchikoo sat down on a small bank of grass to enjoy what he saw.

He was not really much of a connoisseur, the old man. He just knew what he liked when he saw it. The three stones were light brown in color, delicately veined, and so smooth that they almost looked slippery. Old Man Potchikoo began to wonder if they really were slippery, and then he thought of touching them.

They were in the middle of the soft slough mud, so the old man took his boots and socks off. Then he thought of his wife Josette and what she would say if he came home with mud on his clothes. He took off his shirt and pants. He never wore undershorts. Wading toward those stones, he was as naked as them.

He had to kneel in the mud to touch the stones, and when he did this he sank to his thighs. But oh, when he touched the stones, he found that they were bigger than they looked from the shore and so shiny, so slippery. His hands polished them, and polished them some more, and before he knew it that Potchikoo was making love to the slough.

Years passed by. The Potchikoos got older and more frail. One day Josette went into town, and as he always did as soon as she was out of sight, Potchikoo sat down on his front steps to do nothing.

As he sat there, he saw three women walk very slowly out of the woods. They walked across the field and then walked slowly toward him. As they drew near, Potchikoo saw that they were just his kind of women. They were large, their hair was black and very long, and because they wore low-cut blouses, he could see that their breasts were beautiful— light brown, delicately veined, and so smooth they looked slippery.

"We are your daughters," they said, standing before him. "We are from the slough."

A faint memory stirred in Potchikoo as he looked at their breasts, and he smiled.

"Oh my daughters," he said to them. "Yes I remember you. Come sit on your daddy's lap and get acquainted."

The daughters moved slowly toward Potchikoo. As he saw their skin up close, he marveled at how fine it was, smooth as polished stone. The first daughter sank upon his knee and clasped her arms around him. She was so heavy the old man couldn't move. Then the others sank upon him, blocking away the sun with their massive bodies. The old man's head began to swim and yellow stars turned in his skull. He hardly knew it when all three daughters laid their heads dreamily against his chest. They were cold, and so heavy that his ribs snapped apart like little dry twigs.

Windigo

For Angela

*The Windigo is a flesh-eating, wintry demon with a man buried deep inside of it. In
some Chippewa stories, a young girl vanquishes this monster by forcing boiling lard
down its throat, thereby releasing the human at the core of ice.*

You knew I was coming for you, little one,
when the kettle jumped into the fire.
Towels flapped on the hooks,
and the dog crept off, groaning,
to the deepest part of the woods.

In the hackles of dry brush a thin laughter started up.
Mother scolded the food warm and smooth in the pot
and called you to eat.
But I spoke in the cold trees:
New one, I have come for you, child hide and lie still.

The sumac pushed sour red cones through the air.
Copper burned in the raw wood.
You saw me drag toward you.
Oh touch me, I murmured, and licked the soles of your feet.
You dug your hands into my pale, melting fur.

I stole you off, a huge thing in my bristling armor.
Steam rolled from my wintry arms, each leaf shivered
from the bushes we passed
until they stood, naked, spread like the cleaned spines of fish.

Then your warm hands hummed over and shoveled themselves full
of the ice and the snow. I would darken and spill
all night running, until at last morning broke the cold earth
and I carried you home,
a river shaking in the sun.

The Red Sleep of Beasts

On space of about an acre I counted two hundred and twenty of these animals; the banks of the river were covered thus with these animals as far as the eye could reach and in all directions. One may judge now, if it is possible, the richness of these prairies.

—from a letter by Father Belcourt, a missionary
who accompanied the Michif on one
of their last buffalo hunts in the 1840s;
North Dakota Historical Collections, Volume V

We heard them when they left the hills,
Low hills where they used to winter and bear their young.
Blue hills of oak and birch that broke the wind.
They swung their heavy muzzles, wet with steam,
And broke their beards of breath to breathe.

We used to hunt them in our red-wheeled carts.
Frenchmen gone *sauvage*, how the women burned
In scarlet sashes, black wool skirts.
For miles you heard the ungreased wood
Groan as the load turned.

Thunder was the last good hunt.
Great bales of skins and meat in iron cauldrons
Boiling through the night. We made our feast.
All night, but still we could not rest.

We lived headlong, taking what we could
But left no scraps behind, not like the other
Hide hunters, hidden on a rise,
Their long-eyes brought herds one by one
To earth. They took but tongues, and you could walk
For miles across the strange hulks.

We wintered in the hills. Low huts of log
And trampled dirt, the spaces tamped with mud.

At night we touched each other in our dreams
Hearing, on the wind, their slow hooves stumbling

South, we said at first, the old ones knew
They would not come again to the low hills.
We heard them traveling, heard the frozen birches
Break before their long retreat
Into the red sleep.

Turtle Mountain Reservation

For Pat Gourneau, my grandfather

The heron makes a cross
flying low over the marsh.
Its heart is an old compass
pointing off in four directions.
It drags the world along,
the world it becomes.

My face surfaces in the green
beveled glass above the washstand.
My handprint in thick black powder
on the bedroom shade.
Home I could drink like thin fire
that gathers
like lead in my veins,
heart's armor, the coffee stains.

In the dust of the double hollyhock,
Theresa, one frail flame eating wind.
One slim candle
that snaps in the dry grass.
Ascending tall ladders
that walk to the edge of dusk.
Riding a blue cricket
through the tumult of the falling dawn.

At dusk the gray owl walks the length of the roof,
sharpening its talons on the shingles.
Grandpa leans back
between spoonfuls of canned soup
and repeats to himself a word
that belongs to a world
no one else can remember.

The day has not come
when from sloughs, the great salamander

lumbers through snow, salt, and fire
to be with him, throws the hatchet
of its head through the door of the three-room house
and eats the blue roses that are peeling off the walls.

Uncle Ray, drunk for three days
behind the jagged window
of a new government box,
drapes himself in fallen curtains, and dreams that the odd
beast seen near Cannonball, North Dakota,
crouches moaning at the door to his body. The latch
is the small hook and eye.

of religion. Twenty nuns
fall through clouds to park their butts
on the metal hasp. Surely that
would be considered miraculous almost anyplace,

but here in the Turtle Mountains
it is no more than common fact.
Raymond wakes,
but he can't shrug them off. He is looking up
dark tunnels of their sleeves,
and into their frozen armpits,
or is it heaven? He counts the points
of their hairs like stars.

One by one they blink out,
and Theresa comes forth
clothed in the lovely hair
she has been washing all day. She smells
like a hayfield, drifting pollen
of birch trees.
Her hair steals across her shoulders
like a postcard sunset.

All the boys tonight, goaded from below,
will approach her in The Blazer, The Tomahawk,
The White Roach Bar where everyone
gets up to cut the rug, wagging everything they got,
as the one bass drum of The Holy Greaseballs
lights a depth
charge through the smoke.

Grandpa leans closer to the bingo.
The small fortune his heart pumps for
is hidden in the stained, dancing numbers.
The Ping-Pong balls rise through colored lights,
brief as sparrows
God is in the sleight of the woman's hand.

He walks from Saint Ann's, limp and crazy
as the loon that calls its children
across the lake
in its broke, knowing laughter.
Hitchhiking home from the Mission, if he sings,
it is a loud, rasping wail
that saws through the spine
of Ira Comes Last, at the wheel.

Drawn up through the neck ropes,
drawn out of his stomach
by the spirit of the stones that line
the road and speak
to him only in their old agreement.
Ira knows the old man is nuts.
Lets him out at the road that leads up
over stars and the skulls of white cranes.

And through the soft explosions of cattail
and the scattering of seeds on still water,
walks Grandpa, all the time that there is in his hands
that have grown to be the twisted doubles
of the burrows of mole and badger,
that have come to be the absence
of birds in a nest.
Hands of earth, of this clay
I'm also made from.

Louise Erdrich

Tracks

'We started dying before the snow, and like the snow, we continued to fall. It was surprising there were so many of us left to die . . .'

'The direct fierce narrative tells strange stories about Fleur Pillager, who twice drowns in Lake Matchimanito and returns to life to bedevil her enemies. She uses the strength of the black underwaters as a resource against the tribesmen, who are decimated by disease, demoralized by drink, and selling off their forest reserves for a few dollars. *Tracks* leads to a wild world of imagination and sensation.'   *The Times*

'What gives this novel its resonance is Erdrich's extraordinary ability to create not an approximation of the past, but something that seems like a living, breathing evocation of it. The two narrators provide starkly different versions of events. Nanapush is a survivor, wily and adaptable, while Pauline breaks down under the accumulated horrors, eagerly trading the legends of her tribe for those of a Roman Catholic convent. A book of powerful, poetic images, in which myth and reality elide . . . the novel leaves behind an indelible impression.'   *Guardian*

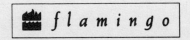